FAMILY WALKS AROUND FARNHAM AND

CONTENTS

Published by
FOOTMARK PUBLICATIONS
12 The Bourne, Fleet, Hampshire

FAMILY WALKS SERIES

Family Walks around Farnham & the Hampshire Borders ISBN 0 9527363 6 5
Family Walks around the Blackwater Valley 2000
Family Walks around Hook, Hartley Wintney & Rotherwick 1999
Family Walks around Odiham & Upton Grey 1998
Family Walks around Fleet & Crookham 1997

Great care has been taken to be accurate. The publisher cannot however accept any responsibility for errors which may occur, or their consequences. All walk descriptions have been checked independently, but changes can occur. **If any problems are encountered on the walks, please report to the relevant Rights of Way Officer asking for the problem to be cleared. Give a map reference if possible.**

Addresses and telephone numbers are:

Rights of Way Officer,
Surrey County Council,
Environment Department,
West House, Merrow Lane,
Guildford GU4 7BQ
Tel: 01483 503151 Ext 7538

Rights of Way Officer,
East Hampshire District Council
Penns Place,
Petersfield,
Hampshire GU32 4EX
Tel: 01730 234388

ABBREVIATIONS

R	Right	SP	Signpost
RHS	Right hand side	S	Stile
L	Left	FB	Footbridge
LHS	Left hand side	W	Waymark

INTRODUCTION

This book covers twelve circular walks in the attractive countryside around Farnham and the Hampshire borders. Some of the walks were included in an earlier Family Walks around Farnham, but these have been revised and seven new walks are included. The usual format of the walk description and accompanying map on facing pages is retained. Paragraph numbers correspond to numbers on the maps. Points of Interest seen on the walks are described separately at the end of the book.

Starting points for the walks (where parking should be available) are shown on a map in the centre pages of the book. However all of the walks can be started from any point on the walk and indeed for some walks alternative start points are indicated. Some walks can be started using train services to Farnham or Bentley stations or bus services to some villages. Ordnance Survey Explorer Maps Nos 144 & 145 at a scale of 2 ½ inches to the mile show all the footpaths used in the walks in detail and allow variations in the walks should this be desired. However the maps included in this book give adequate guidance.

Most of the walks pass public houses where refreshments are available. Please ask the landlord for permission if you wish to leave you car in the pub car park (and remember to use the hospitality!)

In dry conditions good walking shoes should suffice, but wellies may be needed in wetter conditions. Dog owners please keep your dog on a lead where livestock is present and it is probably wisest to avoid fields with livestock and their young.

Some walks pass close to private houses - please respect the residents' privacy.

My thanks to Ted Blackman for his sketch maps (based on out of copyright maps and path surveys) and to the following for checking the new walks: June & Mark Beckley, Carol Coleman & June Beckley, Jane & David Eccles, Pat Sansom and Pam & Steve Turner.

Bob Rose
January 2001

Walk No 1   BINSTED, FROYLE & ISINGTON MILLS

[4 miles, 2 hours]

1. Start from The Cedars, Binsted. Turn L along the road and shortly at Binsted House, turn L at a footpath signpost, follow an enclosed path and cross a small field to reach Binsted Church. Enter Binsted churchyard and go along a gravel path [passing a seat and Montgomery's grave], go through a gap in the hedge and along the RHS of the field. Shortly at a 2-fingered signpost, turn R on a track and in a few yards at another 2-fingered signpost, turn L across a field. Bear R to descend through a gap in the trees and cross a footbridge. Turn R at the 3-fingered signpost, go along the LHS of a long, narrow field to pass a barn. Continue ahead and shortly at a 2-fingered footpath signpost, bear R and then L at another 2-fingered signpost. Go along the LHS of the field, over a stile and the descend the steps to a road.

2. Turn R along the road, in a few yards turn L at a footpath signpost and go along the LHS of the field. At the hedge corner by a waymark post on your L, turn R on a grass path across the field. At Southwold, turn L along the road. Ignore two L turns off the road; about 120 yards beyond the second road, go over a stile on the L by a footpath signpost, follow round the field edge. Go through a gap in the hedge and over a stile on your R. Cross a small field to a stile opposite, descend some steps, cross a railway line with care, up some steps and over a stile. Follow the LHS of the field, over a stile, keep ahead across a large field aiming for a stable roof to reach the road via a stile.

3. Go ahead on the road and over the River Wey, pass Froyle Mill, up a short hill, turn R at a footpath signpost, over a stile to follow the path along the RHS of the large field. At the field corner, go through a gap in the hedge and along an enclosed path to join the road. Turn R along the road and over the River Wey to pass Isington Mill [formerly Field Marshal Montgomery's final residence, but now in private ownership]. Go up the hill and turn L at the T-junction on the road to Bentley, in 200 yards opposite Newton Bungalow, turn R at a footpath signpost and through a gate.

4. Follow the enclosed path under the railway bridge, bear L across the field to a fuel tank. At the 2-fingered signpost, go across the large field. Just beyond the crest of the hill, look out for a 4-fingered signpost on your R by a bush. Turn R across the open field and leave the field by a stile and footbridge. Go along the LHS of the next field [with the wood on your L]; at the corner of the wood [by a waymark post], keep ahead across the field to a gap in the trees by a 3-fingered signpost. Bear L with the trees on your L and follow the track in due course pass a 3-fingered signpost and some wooden pylons to reach a road. Turn R along the road [using the footway] to reach The Cedars pub.

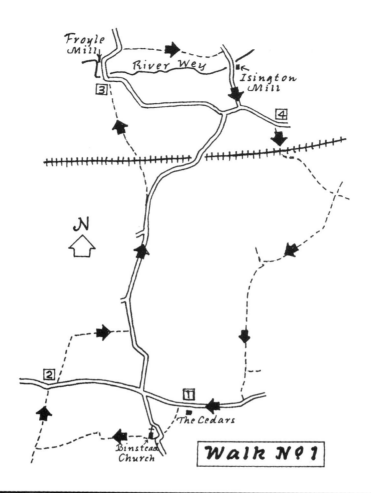

Walk Nº 1

Welcome to "**THE CEDARS**"
BINSTED
Tel: 01420-22112
A Traditional Village Pub
Offering a Warm Welcome

* Families Welcomed * Restaurant * Cask Conditioned Ales * Excellent Food * Functions Catered For * Extensive Beer Garden *Lunch 12-2.30pm

Walk No 2   BENTLEY CHURCH & PAX HILL

[4 miles, 2 hours]

1. Start from Bentley Memorial Hall. Go along the main road passing the Star Inn and shops. Just beyond Red Lion house, pass a footpath signpost on your L, but do not take the footpath. Shortly fork L on a tarmac path along the edge of a green [with a pond on your R]. Turn L up the lane passing a school. At the T-junction, turn L at church sign and soon R at a further church sign and go up the lane to the church.

2. Turn L along the lane away from the church. At the T-junction, turn R on the road and then L at footpath signpost passing Jenkyn Place on your L. Go along a track through two wooden gates and keep along the LHS of a large field. At the end of the field, go through a gap in the hedge and keep along the LHS of the next field. At the end of the field at a 3-fingered signpost, turn L along a track and shortly R on another track that soon follows a tall hedge on your L. Keep along the path enclosed in trees [watch out for cables on your L] to reach a 2-fingered signpost.

3. Turn L on the drive away from Pax Hill School and in 100 yards look out for a 2-fingered signpost on your R. Turn R over a stile and go along the LHS of a large field. Pass a house on your L and at a footpath signpost, go across the large field on a path that continues through trees soon reaching a 3-fingered signpost by some large white posts. Turn L down the drive to reach the road at Coldrey.

4. Cross the road with care and go down the road opposite using the footway. Go under the bridge and round the road to the L. At the end of the metal barrier on your L, turn L down a tarmac path, over a stile by a footpath signpost and along the RHS of a large meadow. Pass between two oak trees and look out for and cross a stile on your R. Turn L along the field edge and soon reach a 3-fingered signpost in the corner of the field.

5. Turn L and cross a footbridge and stile, over a field to a water trough and soon cross a stile by a signpost. Keep along the LHS of the field crossing two adjacent stiles. Stay along the LHS of the large field and at the field corner by a 2-fingered signpost on your L, turn L over stile and along a track on the RHS of a field. At the house, turn R along the drive which becomes The Drift and reach a road. Turn L along the road over the bypass and continue to cross the road with care to return to the start.

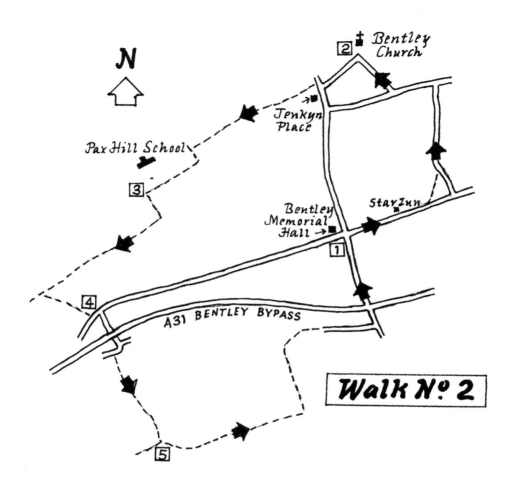

N

Bentley Church

Jenkyn Place

Pax Hill School

[3]

Bentley Memorial Hall →

Star Inn

[1]

[4]

A31 BENTLEY BYPASS

[2]

Walk Nº 2

[5]

STAR INN

BENTLEY, HAMPSHIRE
Telephone: 01420 23184
Full range of food available - Sunday Carvery
OPEN 11am to 3pm and 6pm to 11pm
MONDAY TO SATURDAY
12 noon to 10.30pm on Sundays
As seen on Meridian's 'THE VILLAGE'

Walk No 3 HOME HANGER & RIVER HILL FARM

[5 miles, 2½ hours]

1. Start from Bentley Station [free parking weekends]. Go over the level crossing at the end of the platform. Turn L and follow the tarmac path through the white kissing gates. In about 100 yards at 4-fingered signpost, turn R through a kissing gate onto the path through Bentley Station Meadow. Leave the meadow by a kissing gate close to a 2-fingered signpost. Go ahead along the track, at a 'Private No Public Thoroughfare' notice by the 2-fingered signpost on your L, follow the path parallel to the track [with a wood on your L] Pass a 2-fingered signpost and at a 4-fingered signpost go on the path ahead through the wood to reach a road.

2. Cross the road carefully and turn R, then L at a footpath signpost by Broadview Farm. Go along the drive, fork L and shortly turn R over a stile by a 2-fingered signpost and a metal gate, go along the RH edge of the field. At the second stile, bear half R across a small field to cross the cutting of the disused Bordon Railway. At the top of the bank, cross a stile by a signpost and go ahead up a large field. Near the top of the hill, cross a stile by a gate and continue with a wooden fence on your R to cross a stile in a wire fence.

3. Turn L and keep along the LH edge of the field [with trees and Home Hanger on your L]. At the end of the wood and hanger, go ahead on a track across the field aiming to the R end of a line of trees. Descend on a path with a wire fence on your L. Shortly at the end of the line of conifers, look out for a gap in the trees and bear L a at waymark post, reaching a kissing gate and another gate. Go ahead past stables, through a kissing gate and descend steps to the road at River Hill Farm.

4. Bear L across the road and over a stile by a 2-fingered signpost. Go along the LH edge of the field and at the end of the wooden fence on your L, by the waymark, turn R across the field to a stile in some trees. Follow the enclosed path that shortly goes along the LH edge of a large field. At a 2-fingered signpost, turn L along the field edge and at the field corner, go through a gap by a 2-fingered signpost. Turn R along a track on the RH edge of the field to reach a road.

5. Turn L along the road and in a few yards at a footpath signpost on your R, fork R along a track and in about 50 yards at a 2-fingered signpost turn R on a path across a large field. At a 3-fingered signpost, turn R along the LH edge of field. At the corner of the field keep ahead through some trees and then along the RH field edge to reach a road. [Turn L for The Cedars pub] Turn R along the road and in a few yards cross the road to a signpost opposite and take the track that leads across a large field. Pass a 3-fingered signpost on your L and at the start of a line of trees, turn R at a 3-fingered signpost on a path across a large field.

6. At the end of this long path reach but do not cross the stile seen at the start of paragraph 3 above. Turn L along the RH field edge and at the corner of the field, turn R over a stile by a 3-fingered signpost along the LH edge of the field. Pass a stile on your L but continue ahead to another stile in the corner of the field. Descend on the track through the wood [can be muddy]; at the end of the wood, cross a footbridge and stile and keep ahead passing a signpost and then a 2-fingered signpost. Go across the large field [with a wood on your L], over a stile in a hedge.

7. Cross the road with care to a signpost opposite. Go through the chicane, over the stile and across the field to a stile by a metal gate. Go along the LH field edge and through the white kissing gate to return to Bentley Station.

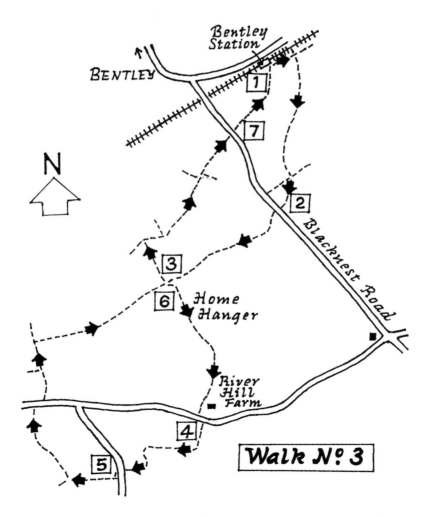

Walk No 4   LOWER OLD PARK & DIPPENHALL

[$4\frac{1}{2}$ miles, $2\frac{1}{4}$ hours]

1.   Start from Farnham Lane Recreation Ground at the end of Dippenhall Street, Crondall. Go about 100 yards along the road away from the village, at a footpath signpost on your L, turn L over a stile in a hedge. Keep along the LH edge of the field, in the field corner, go through a gap in the hedge and turn half R diagonally across the next field to a stile in the corner. Go along the RHS of the golf course, soon pick up an enclosed path and up the hill to cross a stile. At the top of the hill, keep along the RHS of the field, in the field corner go through a gap by a 2-fingered signpost and along the drive to a road.

2.   Turn R along the road [beware traffic], in 250 yards at a footpath signpost on your L, turn L over a stepped stile by a metal gate and across a large field. Enter the wood, descend on the path, over a footbridge and up the slope. Leave the wood by a 2-fingered signpost and go over the field aiming to the L of the house, go through a kissing gate to join the road through Lower Old Park.

3.   Turn R along the road, descend the hill, turn L at the T-junction. At the bottom of the hill, cross a bridge with a brick parapet, turn L through a gate by a signpost along an enclosed path, turn L along a track and pass some houses to reach a road.

4.   Cross the road with care to a signpost opposite, go up the bank, over a stile and straight up across the field to a 3-fingered signpost. Turn R along the grass track, at the farm buildings, follow the enclosed track and through a small wooden gate to reach a road at Dippenhall. Turn L along the road [beware traffic] and shortly fork R at the 'Well and Long Sutton' sign, ignore all side turnings and pass the 'Hampshire' sign. At the Y-junction keep ahead on the Well and Long Sutton road..

5.   In about 50 yards look out for at a footpath signpost on your R, turn R by a white metal barrier along a track. Descend the hill, ignore all side turnings passing houses and Clare Park Farm. At the public road, turn L [beware traffic] and return to the start.

The Plume of Feathers

Walk Nº 4

Croft Lane

Dippenhall Street

Rec Ground

1

S SP

2

SP

S

S

FB

S

Lower Old Park

N

4

SP

SP

SP

Dippenhall

5

Walk No 5   WELL & LORD WANDSWORTH COLLEGE

[4 miles, 2 hours]

1. Start from The Chequers, Well. Go along the Long Sutton road away from the phone box. In 300 yards, opposite the Well village sign, look out for a stile up a bank on your L. Cross the field on a path [signpost] and descend to a stile opposite close to a white post. Turn R along Frog Lane.

2. In $\frac{1}{2}$ mile reach a 5-fingered signpost and turn hard R on a path across the field. At the field corner, go through a gap and along the RH edge of the College sports field to the wooden gates by a waymarked post. Go half L across a tarmac area and then ahead on a tarmac path by another waymarked post. In 300 yards, bear L just before the buildings, cross a car park and follow the tarmac path. At the T-junction, turn R along a footway and shortly turn half L along a path and then L along the road. Leave Lord Wandsworth College by the large ornamental gates.

3. [The Four Horseshoes pub to your L]. Turn R along road and in a few yards turn L at a footpath signpost along the RH edge of the pub play area. Cross two stiles, keep along the RH edge and then across a large field to cross a track and through a gap in the trees. Continue ahead on a path across another large field and reach a 4-fingered signpost in the mid-field. Turn hard R along the path to pass through a gap in the tree line [waymark on oak tree]. Bear half R across the next field to reach Long Lane.

4. Cross the road and go along the road to Stapeley Farm. Just beyond the white house on your R and before entering the yard, turn R up the bank to a footpath signpost. Go along the LH field edge and at the field corner cross a stile. Bear half L across the next large field to cross a stile in the field corner. Bear half R across a further field to reach a stile in a fence at the LH edge of a hedgerow. Bear half L across a small field, up a bank and over a stile to cross another small field to a stile by a new house. Continue and shortly cross a stile and turn R along the road to The Chequers.

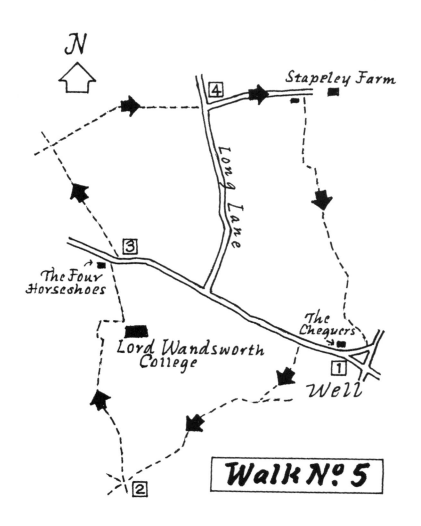

Walk Nº 5

13

Walk No 6   CAESAR`S CAMP & UPPER OLD PARK

[5 miles, 2½ hours]

1. Start from the TO TOILETS signpost in the car park at Farnham Park Golf Course. Follow the tarmac path on the edge of the grassed area passing the brick changing rooms on your L. In about 200 yards, turn L through wooden posts along another tarmac path through trees. Cross a metalled track [by a seat] to the Keeper's Cottage, keep ahead and descend crossing two footbridges over streams. Leave the park by a gap beside a green metal gate. Go ahead on a road between houses and along The Green on the RHS of Hale recreation ground. The Ball & Wicket is opposite.

2. With great care cross the road, turn R and then immediately L up Vicarage Lane. At the top of the lane, turn R and then L up Heath Lane. Cross the road carefully and turn R down Alma Lane. At Beam Cottage, just before The Alma, turn L at a footpath signpost up a track; pass a metal barrier and bear L up a grass track [houses on your L]. At the top of the hill, cross a track and go down the steep track opposite. Keep ahead ignoring crossing tracks; at a T-junction turn R and in 35 yards turn L along a track. Ignore all crossing tracks, just beyond a wooden shelter on your L, fork L.

3. Shortly at another T-junction, turn R and in 25 yards turn L up a steep stoney track [passing a NO ADMITTANCE WATER CATCHMENT AREA notice on your R] to enter Caesar's Camp - an Iron Age hillfort. Bear R along the edge to a clump of trees at the end. Bear L and follow a track along the edge of the escarpment; in 500 yards go through the substantial hillfort earth banks. Turn L along a track, in 130 yards cross a track and in a further 50 yards fork R and R again along a track with a bank on your R. After 150 yards, fork L on a path through trees. In ¼ mile at a T-junction turn L, go over a gravel bank and track, then ahead on a path through bushes [houses on your L] to reach a road.

4. Cross the road with great care to Lawday Link opposite. Go along the footpath on the RHS of the road. Cross a further road carefully and go along Heathyfields opposite [bridleway signpost]. Keep ahead on the track past houses, at a bridleway waymark post go ahead on the road. Shortly at No 19 on your R, go along a metalled path between conifer hedges. Soon cross a track and continue on another track with a paddock on your L.

5. In ¼ mile at Woodside Cottages, turn L along a track and R at Old Park Stables. Continue along a rough track eventually to meet a road. With extreme care cross this road, up the steps and turn L along the path to return to the start.

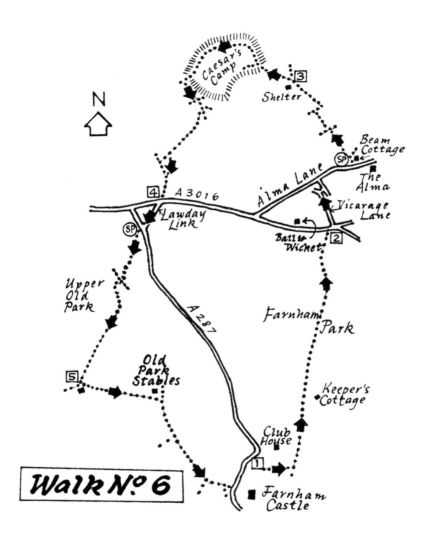

N

Caesar's Camp

3

Shelter

Beam Cottage

SP

The Alma

4 A3016

Alma Lane

Vicarage Lane

Lawday Link

SP

Ball & Wichet

2

Upper Old Park

Farnham Park

A287

Old Park Stables

5

Keeper's Cottage

Club House

1

Walk Nº 6

Farnham Castle

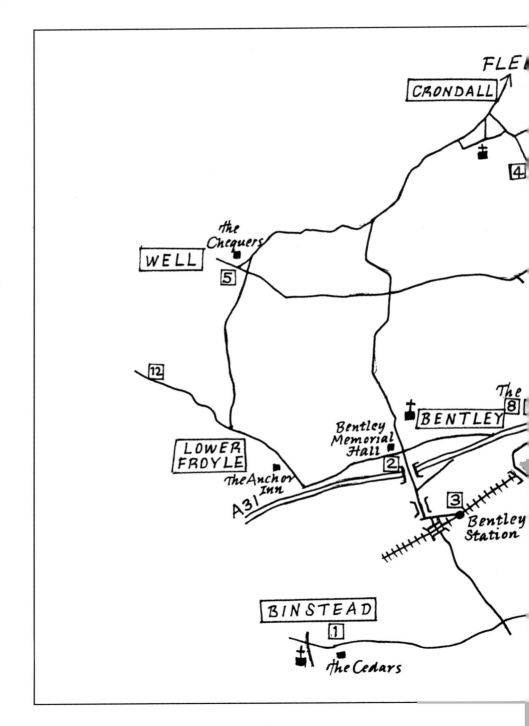

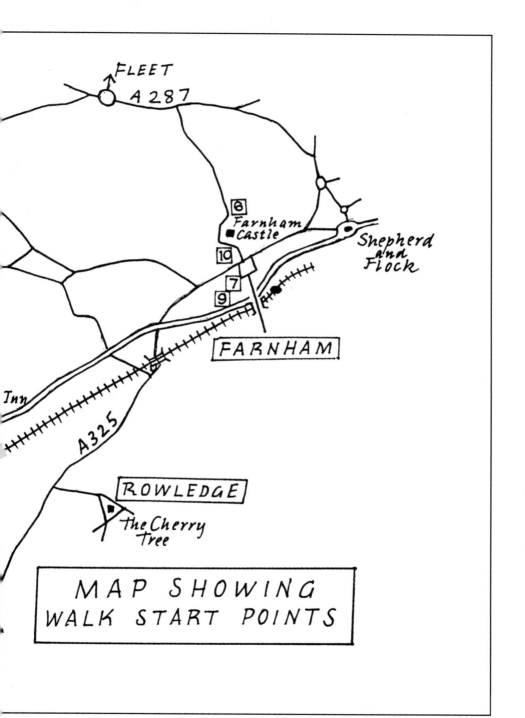

FLEET

A 287

6

Farnham Castle

10

7

9

Shepherd and Flock

FARNHAM

Inn

A325

ROWLEDGE

the Cherry Tree

MAP SHOWING WALK START POINTS

Walk No 7   RIVER WEY & DIPPENHALL

[4 miles, 2 hours]

1. Start from Waggon Yard car park, Farnham. At the New Ashgate Gallery, turn L along the road and enter the churchyard. Fork L on a path leading to an enclosed tarmac path; continue on this path across rough meadows. Turn L at a footbridge and keep on the tarmac path, in 200 yards cross two footbridges and the River Wey. Turn R by Weydon Mill, leave the tarmac path and fork R along the riverside footpath. In 300 yards reach the road..

2. With great care cross the dualled Farnham bypass to a footpath signpost opposite on the R. Follow the path by the river and continue on a lane past houses. In due course reach and cross with great care the busy A325 [a break will come!] to the footpath signpost opposite. Go along the enclosed path and in 300 yards reach a road.

3. Turn R over the River Wey bridge and keep along the RHS of the road [beware traffic] to reach and cross with great care the busy dualled A31. Go along Runwick Lane opposite; just beyond Runwick House, turn L over a stile. Go through the LH metal gate, across the field to another metal gate in a hedge. Continue across the field to a further metal gate. Keep along the RH field edge and reach the road via a stile. Turn L along the road and in 100 yards, turn R along the Dippenhall road, going down then up the lane. Just beyond Dippenhall Grange, turn R at a T-junction.

4. Shortly at Millar's Cottage, turn R along a track, through the small wooden gate and along the enclosed path that bears L to a path along the hillcrest. Pass a 3-fingered signpost and in 400 yards follow the path with the hedge on your L. In the corner of the field, go L through a gap in the hedge, down some steps, over a stile and along the RH field edge. Cross a stile in the field corner, over a track and along an enclosed path opposite. Cross a meadow to another enclosed path opposite, over a footbridge, up the steps leading to a gravel track to reach a road.

5. Cross the road to a footpath signpost opposite and go along Wayneflete Lane. Pass a shop on your R, keep ahead down the road to reach Crondall Lane. Turn R down the road, shortly turn L across the road and along Beavers Close leading to an enclosed path. Turn L along the road, at the school on your R, turn R along the road and shortly at Austin Cottages, turn L along an enclosed path that narrows.

6. At the metal barrier cross the road, turn R at the Public Lavatory sign and along Timber Close to West Street. Turn L along the road, cross at the pedestrian lights, along Church Passage to the churchyard and return to the start.

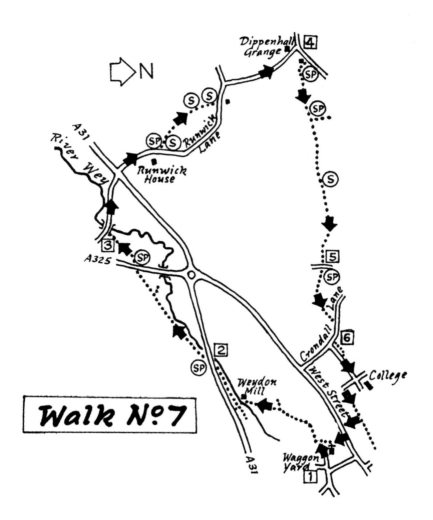

Walk Nº7

Walk No 8   RIVER WEY & ALICE HOLT FOREST

[5 miles, 2½ hours]

1. Start at The Bull Inn, Bentley [park in the layby beyond the pub]. Cross with care the dualled A31 and take Gravel Hill Road opposite. Shortly cross the River Wey bridge, turn L over a stile by a footpath signpost and follow the river bank. After the third stile, follow the wood edge on your R. Continue along the meadow, cross a stile at a footpath signpost, turn R over another stile and go under the railway bridge. Go up the track and then a lane past Holtwood Farm. Just beyond Holt Pound House on your R, turn R at a signpost, go through a kissing gate and across the field to enter the pub garden by squeeze posts. Skirt the edge of The Forest Inn, go through a kissing gate to the road.

2. With great care cross the busy A325 to the footpath signpost opposite the pub [by a post box]. Go along a wide enclosed track; at Glen Cottage brick pillar, ignore the track to the R, and go ahead on the enclosed path. Cross a footbridge, up the path to reach and cross a road. Turn L along the road, pass Forest Glade on your R and turn R along School Road. Beyond The Cherry Tree on your L, turn R up Church Lane and pass Rowledge Church on your R.

3. Enter Alice Holt Forest by a footpath signpost. In 250 yards where five tracks meet, go ahead on an earth path for ¼ mile and then fork L on a gravel track. Ignore side turnings and in ½ mile at a seat where the gravel track bears L, go ahead on a smaller track shortly to reach the road.

4. Cross with extreme care the busy A325 to the gate opposite. Follow the track and in 350 yards [just beyond the overhead cables] where four tracks meet, bear R on a gravel track. Pass Alice Holt Lodge on your R, soon turn L along a metalled road passing a barrier. Just beyond the pond on your L, turn R at a 4-fingered signpost along a gravel track. Keep ahead at a crossing track, pass a car park and reach the road.

5. Turn L along the road, do not take the turn into Holt Pound Inclosure, but in 200 yards where the road bears L, turn R at a footpath signpost and take the path through the wood. Cross with care the railway line using two stiles and descend across the field to a stile by the red-bricked Bentley Mill. Turn R along the road to return to The Bull Inn.

NOTE The Walk can be started from Bentley Station using the path to the pond in paragraph 4.

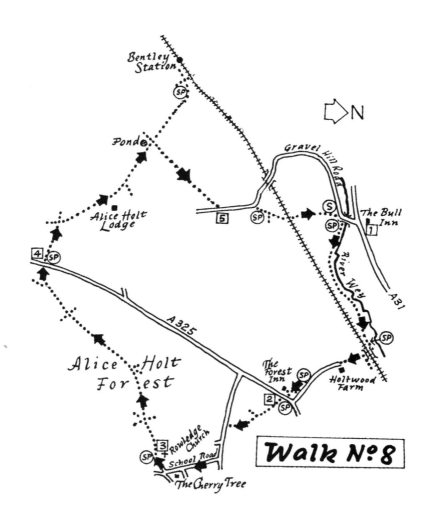

Walk No 8

Walk No 9   NORTH DOWNS WAY and SHEPHERD & FLOCK

[$3\frac{1}{2}$ miles, $1\frac{3}{4}$ hours]

1. Start from the Waggon Yard car park, Farnham. Follow The Maltings sign, leave the car park, do not cross the footbridge over the River Wey, but go on the riverside footpath. Carefully cross the busy road and continue on the riverside footpath. Cross a footbridge, go through Gostrey Meadows and carefully cross the next busy road. Turn R along the footway and very carefully cross the Farnham Bypass using the pedestrian lights.

2. Turn L along the footway at the signpost marking the start of the North Downs Way [note the acorn waymark symbol]. Shortly at a North Downs Way signpost, leave the footway and fork R on a track. In due course pass Snayleslynch Farm; do not enter The Kiln, but turn R along a track under a railway bridge. Follow the footpath with the meadows on your L. Turn L at a North Downs Way signpost and soon turn R over a stile beside an unusual seat. Keep on the footpath [do not fork R uphill] to reach a stile and a road.

3. Turn L along the road and L along Moor Park Lane, over the River Wey and turn L again along a track, still Moor Park Lane. [leave the North Down Ways at the point] Pass Temple Cottage and Kilnside Farm, do not turn L along the footpath to High Mill House. Continue on the track passing under the railway and the road bridges soon to reach the Shepherd and Flock. Go under the subway.

4. Cross over the road to the Bourne Mill and turn L along the footway. Just before the traffic lights, cross the road and turn down Kimbers Lane. Take the footpath [beside the wooden gate] along the riverside. Pass through the car park, turn L on a tarmac path and then R [do not cross the footbridge]. Keep on the riverside footpath, cross the footbridge over the River Wey and continue on the Borelli Walk. Cross the busy road and go through Gostrey Meadow to return to the start.

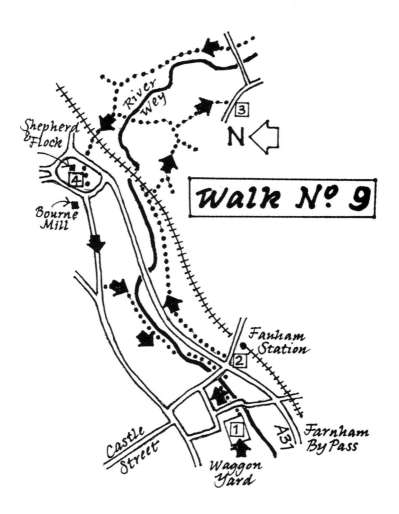

Walk Nº 9

Shepherd & Flock

River Wey

N

3

Bourne Mill

4

Farnham Station

2

A31

Farnham By Pass

Castle Street

1

Waggon Yard

Shepherd & Flock
Free House
Farnham
(01252) 716675

8 Great Ales   Quality Pub Food

The Great Little Pub on the great big roundabout
As featured in the 2001 Good Beer Guide

Walk No 10   FARNHAM PARK & MIDDLE OLD PARK

[4 miles, 2 hours]

1. Start from the Lion & Lamb Yard, Farnham. Go under the brick arches, turn R at the Safeway and along Long Garden Way passing the Hop Blossom to reach and carefully cross Castle Street.   Turn L up the footway passing the Nelson Arms. Keep up the hill and up the flight of Blind Bishop Fox's steps. Fork L to Farnham Park on the path beside the road passing the entrance to Farnham Castle.   Cross the entrance to Farnham Park Golf Course and continue on the enclosed footway beside the road.
Note The Walk can be started from car park at the entrance to Farnham Park.

2. In $\frac{1}{4}$ mile turn R on a tarmac track and over a stile beside a cattle grid. In 150 yards opposite a stile on your R, turn L on a grass path passing a wooden seat. Continue ahead ignoring RH and LH forks, over a footbridge, through squeeze posts and take the LH fork. At the top of the hill pass between two large trees and join an enclosed path to reach a road. Turn L up footway and L again along Drovers Way.

3. At the A 287, turn R and cross the busy road carefully to Upper Old Park Lane opposite. In 200 yards turn L along a track and in about $\frac{1}{4}$ mile turn R at Old Park Stables along a track. In another $\frac{1}{4}$ mile pass Woodside Cottages and keep ahead through a gap to Middle Old Park.

4. Join a tarmac road and in a few yards turn L at a signpost through a kissing gate and along the LHS of a small field. Go through a metal kissing gate, cross a large field on a track and though double metal gates. Turn L along the LHS of a large field. Go through a gap in the field corner, down some steps, over a footbridge and up a path through the woods. Cross a stile and go to the RH corner of the small field. Go over the stile and along an enclosed path that descends and leads eventually to a gap by a stile. Turn L along the LHS of a large field leading to track between houses.

5. Turn R along the road and in 100 yards, turn R at a signpost along an enclosed path. Turn L along the LHS of a field, across another field and down some steps onto a brick path through the College Campus. Bear L through the car park to the start.

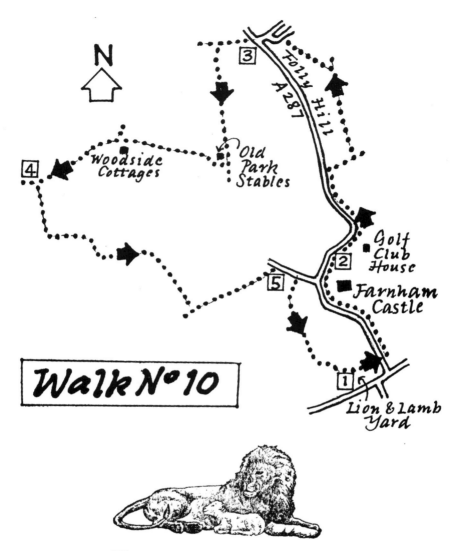

Walk Nº 10

Old Park Stables

Woodside Cottages

Folly Hill

A287

Golf Club House

Farnham Castle

Lion & Lamb Yard

The Lion and Lamb Bistro

Lion and Lamb Yard, West Street, Farnham, Surrey GU9 7LL
Tel & Fax: 01252 715156

Set in an historic courtyard we offer an excellent selection of Home Cooked dishes, freshly prepared sandwiches and baguettes, homemade soup of the day as well as homemade cakes and scones for a traditional Afternoon Tea.
Bookings for groups always welcomed, or just visit for well earned refreshments at the end of your walk.

Walk No 11 RUNWICK LANE & WILLEY MILL

[4 miles, 2 hours]

1. Start at The Bull Inn, Bentley [park in the layby beyond the pub]. Go up the side road by the bus shelter, in a few yards turn R at a footpath signpost, through a kissing gate and along the LHS of the field. Cross the stile in the corner of the field, go along the enclosed path and bear R along a metal lane passing houses to reach a T-junction.

2. Turn R along the winding road, passing Hill Farm on your L. At the oast house, bear L on the road to Wimble Hill. In 200 yards, turn R over a stile by a signpost and go along the RHS of a large field. At the waymark post by the corner of the wood [under pylon wires], go ahead across the field to a stile to the L of a metal gate. Take the enclosed path and go ahead along Runwick Lane. Pass a road turning on your R and in a further ¼ mile, reach a road junction.

3. At this junction, turn R over a stile by a signpost [ignore the metal gate before the stile]. Bear half R across a large field and over a stile 100 yards before the RH field corner. Cross a small field to a further stile. Bear half L across a rough field to a stile in a wire fence; head for the LH corner of the field and cross a stile by Avalon Cottage. Go along a short enclosed footpath, turn L at the bollards along the drive to pass Farnham House Hotel. Continue down the driveway to the A 31.

4. With great care cross the busy dualled carriageway to the footpath signpost to Willey Mill opposite. Enter the driveway and bear R towards the house. Go through a wooden gate beside the house, across the lawn to a further wooden gate and over the footbridge [not the white bridge]. Ignore the LH fork in the path and go ahead across the meadow to a stile. Bear half L across the field passing a small tree to a stile opposite. Go under the railway bridge and turn R along the path. In 300 yards cross a stile and keep ahead, over another stile in a metal gate and along the RHS of the field.

5. Go through a kissing gate, turn R under the railway bridge, over a stile and turn L over another stile by a 3-fingered signpost. Go along the meadow on a path close to the River Wey. Ignore the stile on the LHS before the end of the meadow. Cross two stiles through the wood, through the meadow and over another stile. Cross the final stile by the bridge over the River Wey, turn R along the lane and with great care cross the A 31 to return to The Bull Inn.

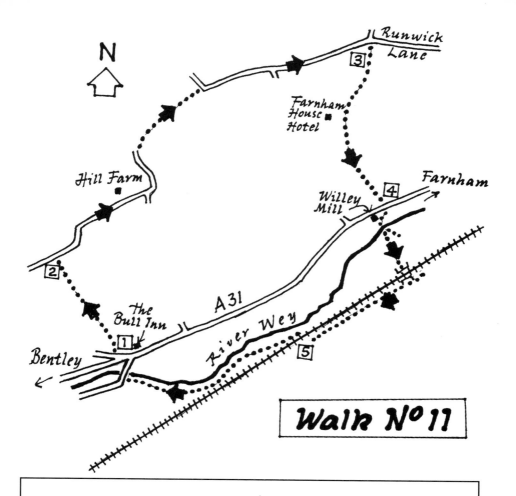

N

Runwick Lane

3

Farnham House Hotel

Hill Farm

Farnham

Willey Mill

4

2

The Bull Inn

A31

River Wey

1

Bentley

5

Walk Nº 11

THE BULL INN

Bentley, Nr Farnham

This traditional English inn will extend you a warm and hearty welcome at the start or finish of your walk.

Pop in for a pint of well kept English ale and a snack or full meal from the extensive choice on our Menus, all prepared and cooked to order.

See you soon

Bill Thompson Innkeeper   Tel: 01420 22156

Walk No 12   SHEEPHOUSE COPSE & HUSSEYS LANE

[4 miles, 2 ¼ hours]

1. Start from the rural layby along the road to the Golden Pot, 1½ mile beyond The Anchor Inn, Lower Froyle. The layby is on the RHS of the road by a bridleway signpost. Go along the bridleway and at the top of the hill, turn R at a 4-fingered signpost along the crest of the hill with Sheephouse Copse on your L. In 600 yards the track bears R at two bridleway signposts; in about another 250 yards pass a metal barrier to reach a road.

2. Cross the road to the bridleway signpost opposite on the L. Go along the bridleway keeping to the edge of the wood on your R. Pass a bridleway notice and in due course arrive at a road.

3. Turn R down the road and at the bottom of the hill where the road turns L, go ahead on Husseys Lane at a byway signpost on your R. Follow this undulating track and in ⅔ mile reach a magnificent viewpoint with a seat on your L in memory of Ken Goschen and his son. In 200 yards just beyond a wooden copse on your R, at a stile and signpost on your R, bear half R across a field towards a stile that comes into view by an elevated yellow marker. Cross the next field to another similarly marked stile. Cross this and an adjacent stile and descend to a further stile. Go along the RHS of the field and just before its corner, go through a gap in the hedge and turn L on a track to reach the road in a few yards.

4. Turn L down the road and in a few yards, turn R over a stile by a signpost. Go along the RHS of the field, in the field corner go through a gap, over a stile and turn L along the LHS of the field. In the field corner, cross a stile and turn L down the drive to the road. Turn R along the road and in ½ mile return to the start.

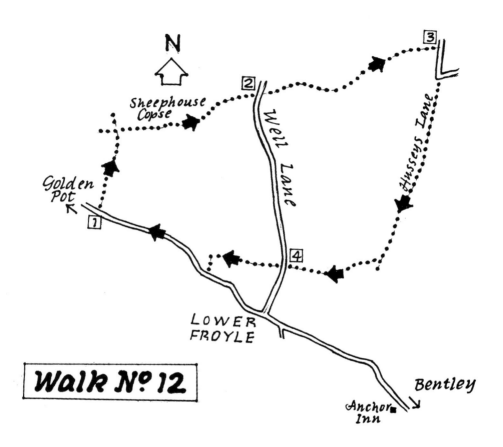

N

Sheephouse
Copse

Well Lane

Hussey's Lane

Golden
Pot

2

3

1

4

LOWER
FROYLE

Bentley

Anchor
Inn

Walk Nº 12

POINTS OF INTEREST

Alice Holt is an ancient woodland. It was the site of a Romano-British pottery works using local timber and clay. Centuries later the forest was owned by Aelfsige, a Saxon Bishop of Winchester. Its name was corrupted over centuries to 'Alice Holt', holt being the old English word for wood. During the Middle Ages it was a royal hunting ground. The forest was maintained for the Government and many oaks were felled for ship-building between the reign of Henry VIII and the Napoleonic Wars. Alice Holt Lodge is a Forestry Commission Research Station and there is a Visitor Centre at Bucks Horn Oak.

[Walk No 8]

Bentley Church was built beside an ancient track that later became the Pilgrims Way between Winchester and Canterbury, the track ran by a holy well near the church . The church is approached through an avenue of yew trees believed to be 600 years old. The yews probably originated when Bentley, which means 'Green by the Forest', supplied an archer to the King each year. The Manor was assigned in the Domesday Book to William the Archer. The original Norman church, now the chancel, was built in the 11th century. The north chapel was added in 1200 and the south chapel in the late 13th century. The 12th century font is made of Purbeck marble.

[Walk No 2]

Binsted Church was probably commenced about 1140 and is dedicated to the Holy Cross. There could have been a Saxon church on or near the site. Benestede as written in the Domesday Book, means a 'holding of land'. The church was extended during the centuries to cater for the increasing population. The tomb of Richard de Westcote, a Crusader, is in the north chapel and has a fine, but battered effigy, c.1320. It was unfortunately damaged early in the 19th century when the chapel was used as a village school and the Crusader's tomb was in the school coal store! Field Marshal the Viscount Montgomery of Alamein was buried in the churchyard on 1st April 1976. He had lived nearby in Isington Mill.

[Walk No 1]

Bordon Light Railway was opened in 1905 and connected Bordon Camp to Bentley Station and hence the railway network. There was an Intermediate Halt at Kingsley. The line was mainly used for military traffic, particularly during both World Wars, but it also served the local community. There was an exchange siding at Bordon to the Longmoor Military Railway with a $3\frac{1}{2}$ mile extension to the Portsmouth line built in 1942. Bordon Light Railway closed in 1966, but there is a well-preserved cutting at Broadview Farm.

[Walk No 3]

Borelli Walk was an idea put forward by Mr C E Borelli for a riverside walk. He died in 1950, but the Farnham Club for the Blind suggested a scented rose garden and with the agreement of Farnham Urban District Council this was opened in 1965 and dedicated to the memory of Mr Borelli who helped to preserve the structural and natural beauties of his native town.

[Walk No 9]

The Bourne Mill is the oldest commercial building in Farnham. It was originally built as a working mill prior to the Domesday listing of 1085. When Farnham Castle was built, its woodland to the north supplied the garrison with charcoal for its gunpowder as well as flour for the town. Its milling function continued into the early part of the twentieth century when it fell into dereliction. It was bought by Farnham Council in 1924 and sold almost derelict in 1959 with only 8 acres of the land it held in 1924. It now is occupied by Bourne Mill Antiques and the mill pond area by Bourne Buildings.   [Walk No 9]

Caesar's Camp is a pre-Roman Iron Age Hill Fort dating from about 500 BC. It lies about 590 ft above sea level and covers 25 acres at the end of a steep-sided spur projecting from a gravel plateau. The fort is a natural strong point protected by the steep sides of the spur fortified by double banks and a deep ditch at the neck of the spur. These features have survived for 2,500 years and are clearly visible from the modern track entering the western end of the fort. The original entrance lies about 150 yards to the east of the modern entrance along the southern escarpment. There is a spring below the ramparts on the north east side that feeds the modern reservoir at Bourley. The hillfort commands a magnificent view; in the foreground: Farnborough Airfield, Long Valley, Farnham and Aldershot; more distantly: the Hog's Back, Guildford Cathedral, Crooksbury Hill, Hindhead and to the north the Thames Valley and beyond with the Chobham Ridges to the north east.

[Walk No 6]

Castle Street has several fine Georgian houses. Adjacent to the Nelson Arms are the oldest buildings, the Windsor Almshouses built in 1619. Further up the hill are the Blind Bishop's Steps. Each flight has seven steps separated by seven paces and enabled Bishop Fox who was blind to find his way unaided to and from his residence in Farnham Castle.   [Walk No 10]

Farnham Castle lies on the historic Harrow Way an ancient trading route from Kent to the West Country. Farnham was an easterly manor of the See of Winchester from Saxon times and it was a convenient stopping place between Winchester and London - a journey the Bishop of Winchester frequently made. Although a Saxon Manor and Christian community flourished in Farnham, the earliest known buildings were begun in 1138 by Henry de Blois, Bishop of Winchester. The first building was the Keep, the ruins which are now looked after by English Heritage. The Great Hall and Norman Chapel date from about 1180. The Castle was occupied in 1216 for a year by the Dauphin. The Castle has had many alterations over the centuries; most prominent is the red brick tower gateway erected by Bishop Wayneflette between 1470 and 1475. This is now known as Fox's Tower after the blind Bishop Fox who modified the tower. The Castle was occupied by Parliamentary forces in the Civil War and subsequently the Keep was slighted on Cromwell's orders - the stones were used by citizens to repave the town. In 1927 Farnham was transferred to Guildford Diocese and the Castle became the residence of the Bishop of Guildford until 1956. The Overseas Service College took over the Castle in 1962 under a lease until 2022.   [Walk Nos 6 & 10]

Farnham Park or the New Park was founded in 1376 by the Bishop of Winchester as one of two deer parks for hunting, the other being the Old Park to the west of the present A 287. Chalk was also extracted from the park for agriculture and clay for pottery. Green glazed Farnham pottery was famous in medieval England. During the Civil War, Parliamentary troops were billeted in the park. In 1643 Royalist troops unsuccessfully attempted to recapture the Castle from encampments above the park. After the Civil War the castle and park were in ruins. The deer were killed and squatters moved in to the park. With the restoration of the monarchy in 1660, Bishop Morley sold the Old Park and reintroduced deer to the New Park. He built the Ranger s House in the centre of the park and it remained the keeper's residence until the 20th Century. Farnham Park was sold to the town of Farnham in 1930.

[Walk No 10]

Gostrey Meadow in the late 17th century was part of an estate owned by the Bush Hotel. Over the years the estate was broken up and by the early 1900s the area was waste land and became a rubbish dump. In 1908, Farnham Urban District Council bought 3 acres of land to use as a public recreation ground. The public donated further money and the site was cleared and levelled; footpaths, fencing, gates and a bridge over the River Wey were provided. Local people gifted trees, plants, seats, a children's swing and a drinking fountain. Gostrey Meadow was opened in 1910. The War Memorial was erected in 1919 and services are held there every year on Remembrance Sunday. During the Second World War the site was used as a British Restaurant and served hundreds of meals daily. Entrance gates were erected to commemorate the Coronation of Her Majesty Queen Elizabeth II on 2nd June 1952.

[Walk No 9]

Lord Wandsworth College, Long Sutton was founded by Sidney James Stern, Baron Wandsworth, a bachelor merchant banker who had been an MP. On his death in 1912, the greater part of his fortune was left to trustees for the education of children deprived of one or both parents. The College in a 1200 acre estate was opened in 1922 for Foundationers concentrating on teaching boys agricultural skills for farm work. In 1957 the College became a public school and has since developed a good academic reputation, but still one quarter of the pupils are Foundationers.

[Walk No 5]

River Wey (north branch) flows from Alton to Farnham with the Pilgrims Way nearby. There were many mills along the river, some remain: Froyle Mill, Isington Mill (the last residence of Field Marshal Montgomery), Turk's Mill, Willey Mill, Weydon Mill in Farnham and High Mill House. Weydon Mill was demolished in 1919, but there is a model of the mill in Farnham Museum. All mills are now in private ownership. [Walk Nos 1, 7, 8, 9 & 11]

Rowledge village straddles the Hampshire and Surrey border and takes its name from Rowditch or in Victorian times 'Rough Ditch' which marked the county border. It was a lawless place and in the 1860s, Revd Henry Jullus, Vicar of Wrecclesham, suggested creating an ecclesiastical parish on both sides of the county border. As the whole area was part of the Winchester Diocese, the Bishop of Winchester agreed. St James Church was built in 1869/70 and the village began to take on its separate identity.

[Walk No 8]